PAULA J. FOX

Heart
of a
Mother

The
Beauty of
a Mother's
Love

Published by Simple Truths
1952 McDowell Road
Suite 300
Naperville, Illinois 60563
800-900-3427

Design and production: Koechel Peterson & Associates, Inc., Minneapolis, MN and Lynn Harker of Simple Truths.

Cover and inside artwork by Katia Andreeva. Artwork designs are reproduced under license from Koechel
Peterson & Associates, Minneapolis, MN, and may not be reproduced without permission.

Printed in the United States of America

ISBN 978-1-60810-153-5

01 WOZ 12

Table of Contents

beauty³

My Mother's Garden

My Mother kept a garden,
a garden of the heart;
She planted all the good things
that gave my life its start.

She turned me to the sunshine
and encouraged me to dream ...
fostering and nurturing
the seeds of self-esteem.

And when the winds and rains came,
she protected me enough …
but not too much—she knew I'd need
to stand up strong and tough.

Her constant good example
always taught me right from wrong …
markers for my pathway
to last my whole life long.

I am My Mother's Garden.
I am her legacy.
And I hope today she feels the *love*
reflected back from me.

AUTHOR UNKNOWN

If I had a single *flower*

for every time I think about you,

I could walk forever in my *garden.*

CLAUDIA GHANDI

fragrance

I want to be like her...
a well-watered garden whose FRAGRANCE
causes all around to breathe in...deeply.

KIMBER ANNIE ENGSTROM

Mothers and Flowers

Every Mother loves flowers...It's as if something within the very depths of her heart is attuned to the beauty and fragrance of nature. Mothers have an affinity for all things beautiful, and as a result, they bring with them a touch of beauty to their world.

Many Mothers find joy in working the soil, planting seeds and nurturing them as they grow into lovely gardens. Others use flowers to decorate their homes with an element of natural beauty, creating an atmosphere of warmth and tranquility. This Motherly instinct to nurture and produce something beautiful extends to her family as well.

Your family and your love must be cultivated like a garden. Time, effort and imagination must be summoned constantly to keep it flourishing and growing.

JIM ROHN

Flowers are often the focus of paintings, fabrics and other accessories that adorn a Mother's life. The fragrances of the most popular body lotions and perfumes are scented to remind us of flowers as well. Mothers and flowers just naturally go together.

Mothers are also a lot LIKE flowers in many ways...each one has her own unique beauty and each is designed by God to bloom where she is planted. As the heart of a Mother grows and blossoms in beauty and grace, she spreads her fragrance of LOVE not only in her home, but throughout her world.

If we make our goal to live a life of compassion and unconditional love, then the world will indeed become a GARDEN where all kinds of flowers can bloom and grow.
ELIZABETH KUBLER-ROSS

Walk with me now through this enchanting garden as we examine how the different qualities and characteristics of each of these flowers remind us of the BEAUTY of a Mother's love.

love

Baby's Breath

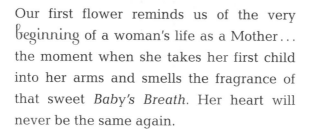

Our first flower reminds us of the very *beginning* of a woman's life as a Mother... the moment when she takes her first child into her arms and smells the fragrance of that sweet *Baby's Breath*. Her heart will never be the same again.

The moment a child is born, the Mother is also born. She never existed before. The woman existed, but the Mother, never. A Mother is something absolutely new.

Bhagwan Shree Rajneesh

Adoption is when a child grew in its Mommy's *heart* instead of her tummy.

AUTHOR UNKNOWN

I think what surprised me the most about Motherhood, as sentimental as it sounds, is how much I *love* my kids. I mean, I just can't believe it. It's like a whole new dimension in emotion that I've never experienced.

GWYNETH PALTROW

beginning

Motherhood is a partnership with God.

HAROLD LUNDSTROM

There is an enduring tenderness in the **LOVE** of a Mother to a son
that transcends all other affections of the heart.

WASHINGTON IRVING

Rose

The *Rose* symbolizes a *Mother's* love for her child.
When a woman becomes a Mother, she experiences
a depth of emotion that she has never known before.
There is no greater love on earth than the love in a
Mother's heart for her child.

*Before I had kids, I never fathomed how much I could actually
love someone. But the LOVE that poured from my soul when I
first held that precious, sleeping baby could not be matched.*

POLLY BENSON

Not until I became a Mother did I understand how much my Mother had sacrificed for me.

Not until I became a Mother did I feel how hurt my Mother was when I disobeyed.

Not until I became a Mother did I know how proud my Mother was when I achieved.

Not until I became a Mother did I realize how much my Mother *loved* me.

VICTORIA FARNSWORTH

With every child, your heart grows bigger and stronger...
There is no limit to how much or how many people you can love...
You just love even more

YASMIN LE BON

Maternal love: a miraculous substance,
which God multiplies as He divides it.

VICTOR HUGO

love

Motherhood: All LOVE begins and ends there.

ROBERT BROWNING

Love is not measured by what it gets, but by what it costs.

OSWALD CHAMBERS

Dogwood

The *Dogwood* is a picture of the *sacrifice* of a Mother's love. It is her great love for her child that enables her to willingly sacrifice "self" and give up her right to personal freedom in order to care for her baby.

*It is not true that love makes all things easy.
It makes us choose what is difficult.*

GEORGE ELIOT

"Mother" means selfless devotion,
limitless *sacrifice*, and love that
passes understanding.

AUTHOR UNKNOWN

Before you were conceived, I wanted you.

Before you were born, I loved you.

Before you were here an hour, I would die for you.

This is the **miracle** of life.

MAUREEN HAWKINS

sacrifice

Duty makes us do things well,
but love makes us do
them beautifully.

ZIG ZIGLAR

The loveliest masterpiece of the
heart of God is the heart of a Mother.

ST. THERESE OF LISIEUX

forgiveness

A Mother's love has the ability to FORGIVE
even the most difficult child.

AUTHOR UNKNOWN

Lilac

The *Lilac* represents the fragrance of a Mother's sacrifice... the lovely scent of *forgiveness* that results when a flower is crushed and gives back to the very one that crushed it. It reminds us of the beauty that surrounds a Mother who is always willing to forgive her children's faults and offer them compassion, mercy and unconditional love.

You may have others who will be more demonstrative but never who will love you more unselfishly than your Mother or who will be willing to do or bear more for your good.

CATHERINE BRAMWELL BOOTH

A child needs your love most when he deserves it the least.

ERMA BOMBECK

To *forgive* is to cultivate a garden filled

with the flowers of kindness and tenderness.

KAREN KINGSBURY

Criticism speaks to the fault with the person;
Love speaks to the person behind the fault.

HENRY JAMES BORYS

forgiveness

The heart of a Mother is a deep abyss at the bottom of which you will always find FORGIVENESS.

HONORÉ DE BALZAC

True Mothers have to be made of steel to withstand
the difficulties that are sure to beset their children.

RACHEL BILLINGTON

Gladiola

It takes a lot of *Strength* to be a Mother, illustrated by the *Gladiola*... a strong powerful flower that is a favorite in large arrangements because of its size. The name Gladiola comes from a Greek word meaning "sword," reminding us that a Mother is a powerful force for her children. She is their advocate, always on their side, and is willing to fight for them against all adversity.

There is nothing so strong as the force of love;
There is no love so forcible as the love of an
affectionate Mother to her child.

ELIZABETH GRYMESTON

strength

*A child's
hand in yours –
what tenderness
and power it arouses.
You are instantly
the very touchstone
of wisdom and
STRENGTH.*

MARJORIE HOLMES

29

A mother's heart is a portrait of "*fighting love*" that will not stop beating for what is best for her children. She is a valiant warrior who will never quit hoping, helping or believing.

JILL RHODES

A Mother's love for her children is like nothing else in the world. It knows no law, no pity; it dares all things and crushes down remorselessly all that stands in its path.

AGATHA CHRISTIE

*Sometimes the STRENGTH
of Motherhood is greater
than natural laws.*

BARBARA KINGSOLVER

strength

The greatest gifts you can give your children are
ROOTS of responsibility and wings of independence.

DENIS WAITLEY

Hydrangea

The *Hydrangea* has a wonderful quality of being able to change color from shades of pink to blue. Initially it was thought that this flower was like a chameleon, changing color to match its surroundings, but experiments proved that the color is actually determined by the *roots* of the plant and the kind of soil it is planted in. This illustrates the Mother who gives her children a rich foundation of love and deep roots of character and strength.

Children are not casual guests in our home. They have been loaned to us temporarily for the purpose of loving them and instilling a foundation of values on which their future lives will be built.

JAMES DOBSON

foundation

$\mathcal{M}$y Mother is my ROOT, my foundation. She planted the seed that I base my life on, and that is the belief that the ability to achieve starts in your mind.

MICHAEL JORDAN

A mother's love provides the best FOUNDATION for building strong character in her children so they will be able to stand against the winds of adversity.

AUTHOR UNKNOWN

You're a foundation builder…
What could be more important than helping
to shape and mold others' lives?

Guy Rice Doud

memories

Mothers write on the hearts of their children
what the rough hand of the world cannot erase.

AUTHOR UNKNOWN

Magnolia

The *Magnolia* blossom grows up high on a huge tree, popular in the South, and is among the first of the flowering plants. Fossil magnolias, imprinted with the image of Magnolia blossoms, have been found that date back to the time of dinosaurs. This flower represents the memories that Mothers imprint on the hearts of their children...a heritage of love that is passed down from one generation to the next.

There is no more influential or powerful role on earth than a Mother's ...
Her words are never fully forgotten, her touch leaves
an indelible impression, and the memories
of her presence lasts a lifetime.

CHUCK SWINDOLL

memories

There is nothing higher and stronger and more wholesome and useful for life in later years than some good memory, especially a memory connected with childhood, with home. Those who carry many such memories with them into life are safe to the end of their days.

Fyodor Dostoevsky

To be in your children's MEMORIES tomorrow, you have to be in their lives today.

BARBARA JOHNSON

I hope my children look back on their childhood and giggle.
I hope I look back on their childhood and smile
because of the memories we have made.

Author unknown

A peaceful Mother is like a medicinal balm.
PEACE and assurance of a Mother's love are
necessary ingredients for a happy home.

WANDA E. BRUNSTETTER

Water Lily

This beautiful *Water Lily* was designed by God to be a picture of tranquility as it floats serenely on top of the water. It represents the quiet beauty of a Mother who creates for her family a safe place of security, comfort and *peace*...a place where they can rest in the knowledge that they are loved and accepted.

One day your children should be able to look back and say,
"My family was the one place where I felt
I could be myself and be loved for it."

BILL HYBELS

A Mother's love is like an island in life's ocean vast and wide. A peaceful, quiet shelter from the restless, rising tide.

HELEN STEINER RICE

41

Peace does not mean to be in a place where there is no noise, trouble or hard work. Peace means to be in the midst of all those things and still be calm in your heart.

Catherine Marshall

A mother is the truest friend we have, when trials heavy and sudden, fall upon us; when adversity takes the place of prosperity; when friends who rejoice with us in our sunshine desert us; when trouble thickens around us, still will she cling to us, and endeavor by her kind precepts and counsels to dissipate the clouds of darkness, and cause PEACE to return to our hearts.

WASHINGTON IRVING

Mom, as often as I come back to your door,
your love meets me on the threshold, and your
serenity gives me comfort and *peace*.
GARY BAUER

Peace

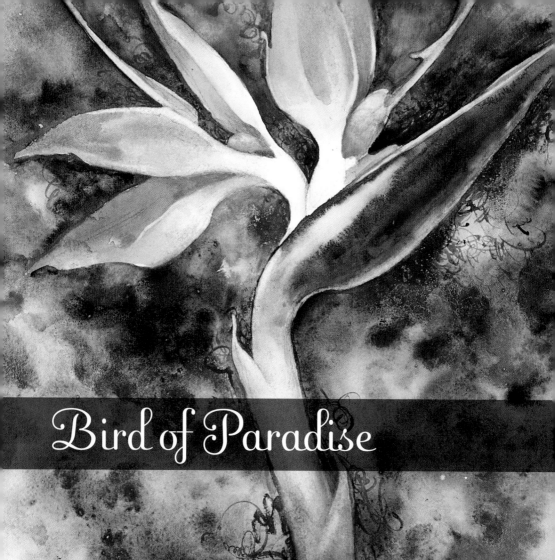

Bird of Paradise

A Mother knows the loving art of always giving with the heart.
She gives her children special things,
like love and wisdom, roots and WINGS.

AUTHOR UNKNOWN

God created the *Bird of Paradise* to actually look like a beautiful bird in flight, reminding us that a wise Mother not only gives her children roots, but she also gives them wings to fly on their own. She helps them develop the confidence and belief in themselves to succeed in life.

Children are not so different from kites. Children were created to fly. But they need wind, the undergirding, and strength that comes from unconditional love, encouragement and prayer.

GIGI GRAHAM TCHIVIDJIAN

"Come to the edge," [she] said.

They said, "We are afraid."

"Come to the edge," [she] said.

They came. [she] pushed them ... And they *flew*.

GUILLAUME APOLLINAIE

The push was the greatest gift she had to offer.
It was her supreme act of love.

DAVID MCNALLY

It is not what you do for your children but what you have taught them to do for themselves that will make them successful human beings. ~ *Ann Landers*

wings to fly

A Mother is not a
person to lean on,
but a person to make
leaning unnecessary.

DOROTHY CANFIELD FISHER

We tend to forget that happiness doesn't come
as a result of getting something we don't have,
but rather of recognizing and appreciating what we do have.

FREDERICK KOENIG

Peony

The name of this gorgeous flower, the *Peony*, comes from the Greek word "paean" meaning "hymn of praise." What a beautiful picture it gives us of the Mother whose life is filled with gratitude and joy. She always sees her cup as half full rather than half empty and is an inspiration and encouragement to others in her world.

Our inner happiness depends not on what we experience but on the degree of our gratitude to God, whatever the experience.

ALBERT SCHWEITZER

$\mathcal{G}$ratitude *unlocks the fullness of life.*
It turns what we have into enough, and more ...
It can turn a meal into a feast, a house into
a home, a stranger into a friend.

MELODY BEATTIE

It is always possible to be thankful for what is given rather than to complain about what is not given. One or the other becomes a habit of life.

ELISABETH ELLIOT

$\mathcal{H}$ow wonderful it would be if we could help our children and grandchildren to learn thanksgiving at an early age. Thanksgiving opens the doors. It changes a child's personality ... Thankful children want to give, they radiate happiness ... they draw people.

Sir John Templeton

Gratitude

Daylily[3]

The *Daylily* get its name from the fact that although the plants themselves bloom for weeks, each blossom lasts only one day. We are reminded of the Mother who lives *each day* to the fullest as if it were her last. She finds joy and creates beauty in the present moments with her children, rather than regretting the past or fearing what the future may bring.

When your life comes to a close, you will remember not days but moments. Treasure each one.

BARBARA JOHNSON

53

each day

*The more time you give to something, the more
you reveal its importance and value to you.*

RICK WARREN

⚜

*I hope my children look back on today,
and see a Mom who had time to play.
There will be years for cleaning and cooking,
for children grow up while we're not looking.*

AUTHOR UNKNOWN

Make *each day* your masterpiece.

JOHN WOODEN

Mothers are like fine collectibles . . .
as the years go by they increase in VALUE.

AUTHOR UNKNOWN

Orchid

The *Orchid* is considered one of the loveliest and most valuable of flowers and symbolizes the Mother who is highly *valued*, not for her external features or material possessions, but for her beautiful character qualities...and the generous love and care she gives to her children over the years.

Most of all the other beautiful things in life come in twos and threes, by dozens and hundreds. Plenty of roses, stars, sunsets, rainbows, brothers and sisters, aunts and cousins, but only one Mother in the whole wide world.

KATE DOUGLAS WIGGIN

valued³

A Mother is she who can take the place of all others but whose place no one else can take.

Cardinal Mermillod

Children are the true connoisseurs.
What is precious to them has no price – only *value*

Bel Kaufman

The people who are most VALUED are those who add value to others.

AUTHOR UNKNOWN

*Y*ou may have tangible wealth untold; Caskets of jewels and coffers of gold. Richer than I you can never be ... I had a Mother who read to me.

STRICKLAND GILLILAN

No joy in nature is so sublimely affecting as the JOY of
a Mother at the good fortune of her child.

JEAN PAUL RICHTER

Sunflower

Sunflowers remind us of joy... such bright happy flowers ... and the secret of their joy is that they always face the sun. This flower represents the Mother who looks for the bright side in every situation. She has a positive attitude in life, preferring to focus on her blessings rather than her problems.

Taking joy in life is a woman's best cosmetic.

Rosalind Russell

joy

There is a difference between happiness and joy. Happiness is a changing emotion. JOY is a choice you make each day.

AUTHOR UNKNOWN

A happy child has a joyful Mother.

Wanda E. Brunstetter

Tucking Ned in bed one night, I leaned down to kiss him good night. Looking closely at my face, a delighted smile spread over his. "It looks just like sunshine," he said. "What looks like sunshine?" I asked. And his fingers gently touched the lines going out from the corners of my eyes. With such an observation, how could anyone mind growing old?

Ruth Bell Graham

What sunshine is to flowers, smiles are to humanity. They are but trifles, to be sure, but scattered along life's pathway, the good they do is inconceivable.

JOSEPH ADDISON

joy³

Making the decision to have a child is momentous.
It is to decide forever to have your HEART
go walking around outside your body.

ELIZABETH STONE

Anemone

Anemones are gorgeous flowers that come in deep rich shades of red and purple, reminding us of a Mother's *heart* of love that is always beating for her children. Her life is forever interwoven with theirs by invisible cords of affection, and she feels every joy and heartache they experience.

There is no other closeness in human life like the closeness between a Mother and her baby – chronologically, physically, and spiritually they are just a few heartbeats away from being the same person.

SUSAN CHEEVER

heart

God sends us children for another purpose than merely to keep up the race—to enlarge our hearts and to make us unselfish and full of kindly sympathies and affections.

MARY HOWITT

The best and most beautiful things in the world cannot be seen or even touched. They must be felt with the heart.

HELEN KELLER

May a Mother never find herself so busy that she sees herself as being performance-based and not HEART-based.

AUTHOR UNKNOWN

Azalea

Whatever you do, put romance and ENTHUSIASM
into the lives of your children.

MARGARET R. MACDONALD

A blooming *Azalea* bush can range in color from bright red to fuchsia and is often described with terms such as "fiery" and "flaming." It gives us a picture of the Mother who is on fire with a spirit of passion and enthusiasm for life. She gives off sparks that ignite and inspire her children to live their lives with purpose and a sense of adventure ... to never be afraid to stretch their boundaries and achieve their dreams.

Mother love is the fuel that enables a normal human being to do the impossible.

MARION GARRETTY

Nothing great was ever achieved without enthusiasm.

RALPH WALDO EMERSON

❦

We act as though comfort and luxury were
the chief requirements in life, when all we
need to make us really happy is something
to be enthusiastic about.

CHARLES KINGSLEY

Teach your children to embrace life as an
experience filled with endless possibilities
for positively affecting the quality of their
lives and for transforming the world.

STEVEN CARR REUBEN

enthusiasm

Queen Anne's Lace

Queen Anne's Lace is sometimes nicknamed "Bird's Nest" for its nest-like appearance, and, in the symbolism of flowers, it represents a sanctuary or refuge … a home. According to legend, Queen Anne, the wife of King James I, was creating lace as beautiful as a flower when she pricked her finger. The very faint red flower in the center of the white blossoms represents a droplet of her blood, symbolizing for us a Mother's love … the very HEART of the home.

I once asked one of my smaller children what he thought a home was and he replied, "It's a place where you come in out of the rain." The home should be a warm sanctuary from the storms of life for each member of the family. A haven of love and acceptance.

GIGI GRAHAM TCHIVIDJIAN

Home

Calm and peaceful, the *home* should be the one place
where people are certain they will be welcomed,
received, protected and loved.

ED YOUNG

Bring LOVE into your home, for this is where
our love for each other must start.

MOTHER TERESA

The most important work you and I will ever do
will be within the walls of our own HOMES.

HAROLD B. LEE

The woman who creates and sustains a *home* and under

whose hands children grow up to be strong and pure men

and women, is a creator second only to God.

HELEN HUNT JACKSON

COURAGE arises from those who
place the needs of others before themselves.

JEFF O'LEARY

Forsythia

A *Forsythia* bush asserts itself every spring with brilliant blasts of yellow blossoms. It stands out as a very bold and vibrant plant, reminding us that a Mother's love empowers her with strength to face the challenges in her life and the lives of her children with courage and perseverance.

Courage doesn't always roar. Sometimes courage is the quiet voice at the end of the day saying, "I will try again tomorrow."

MARY ANNE RADMACHER

Being deeply loved by someone gives you strength, while loving someone deeply gives you COURAGE.

LAO TZU

The truly courageous person is the one who is ready to sacrifice his desires for the sake of something greater.

ANTHONY DESTEFANO

There is no couıage *like that of a Mother who is protecting and defending her own babies.*

AUTHOR UNKNOWN

No language can express the power and beauty and heroism and majesty of a Mother's love. It shrinks not where man cowers, and grows stronger where man faints.

E. H. Chapin

courage

79

A smile of encouragement at the right moment
may act like SUNLIGHT on a closed-up flower.

PAM CARPENTER

Daisy

The *Daisy* is a happy little flower that got its
name, "day's eye," from the Anglo-Saxons because the original little English daisy closes at
nightfall and opens again at sunrise. This illustrates the day-to-day life of the Mother who
chooses to be a light of encouragement in her
home. She is a daily source of happiness and joy
for her family.

My childhood home was the home of a woman with a genius
for inventing daily life, who found happiness
in the simplest of gestures.

LAURA FRONTY

It was only a sunny smile, and little it cost in the giving.
But like morning light, it scattered the
night, and made the day worth living.

F. SCOTT FITZGERALD

𝒜 Mother's happiness is like a beacon, lighting up the future but reflected also on the past in the guise of fond memories.

Honore de Balzac

Help us to be the always hopeful gardeners of the Spirit
who know that ... without light nothing flowers.

MAY SARTON

light

Delphinium

The name *Delphinium* comes from the Greek word for dolphin because it is shaped like the nose of the bottlenose dolphin. This large creature moves with such grace in the water, reminding us of the beautiful *grace* of a Mother's love…always treating others with kindness, dignity and respect even when they least deserve it.

RECIPE FOR A LOVING MOTHER

Take a large bowl of Grace *. Sprinkle with kindness.*
Add a dash of smiles and a heap of love. Throw in a dash of
forgiveness and a splash of gentleness for flavor. Stir together
throughout the years. Serves innumerable children.

STEPHANIE MICHELE

❧

A Mother is a person who seeing there are only
four pieces of pie for five people, promptly
announces she never did care for pie.

TENNEVA JORDAN

Treating others with Grace is like spackle for

the soul ... It covers over faults and weaknesses

and fills up holes in the heart.

PAULA J. FOX

grace

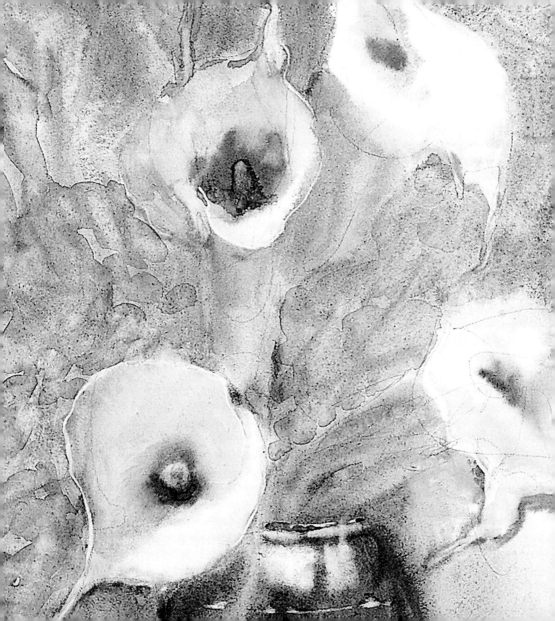

A Mother's arms are made of tenderness
and children sleep soundly in them.
VICTOR HUGO

Calla Lily

The *Calla Lily* gets its name from the Greek word "kalos" meaning "beautiful." It illustrates the beauty of a Mother's love that wraps itself like a protective covering around her children. The white part is actually the bract of the flower...which is usually the green leaf-like underpinning that holds the blossom...and in this case it shelters the flowers inside, just as a Mother provides security and *protection* for her children.

A Mother's love is like a fortress and we seek protection there

When the waves of tribulation seem to drown us in despair.

HELEN STEINER RICE

*A Mother never quite leaves her children at home,
even when she doesn't take them along.*

MARGARET CULKIN BANNING

❧

*They might not need me... but they might.
I'll let my head be just in sight. A smile as small
as mine might be... Precisely their necessity.*

EMILY DICKINSON

protection

We have a choice.
We can choose to have a life full of frustration and fear,
but we can just as easily choose one of joy and CONTENTMENT.

DENNIS SWANBERG

Lupine

This beautiful little purple flower called *Lupine* grows wild in the Arizona deserts, thriving in the poorest of soil. It is a picture of the Mother who has learned to be content in all circumstances, displaying amazing beauty and grace regardless of the situation. Her children learn contentment from her example, and though they may not always have worldly riches, they experience a wealth of blessings.

A rich child often sits in a poor Mother's lap.

SPANISH PROVERB

contentment

The wise Mother teaches her children that
contentment is not the fulfillment
of what you want, but the realization
of how much you already have.

AUTHOR UNKNOWN

A positive mom doesn't take away her children's troubles; she teaches them how to look for the hand of God in the midst of them.

KAROL LADD

Contentment *is appreciating the
beauty of the stars in the night sky.*

AUTHOR UNKNOWN

contentment

True riches are found not in the abundance of things, but in the abundance of gratitude and CONTENTMENT.

AUTHOR UNKNOWN

You can take no credit for beauty at sixteen.
But if you are beautiful at sixty, it will be your soul's own doing.

MARIE STOPES

Zinnia

The early nickname for the *Zinnia* was "youth and old-age" because old flowers stayed fresh even as new flowers on the same stalk began to bloom. It is a reminder that a Mother's physical features may change through the years, but her inner beauty becomes even more beautiful with time.

Some people, no matter how old they get, never lose their beauty...
they merely move it from their faces into their hearts.

MARTIN BUXBAUM

People are like stained-glass windows. They sparkle and shine
when the sun is out, but when the darkness sets in,
their true beauty is revealed only if
there is a light from within.

ELISABETH KUBLER-ROSS

People who possess a true *inner beauty*,

their eyes are a little brighter ... They vibrate at

a different frequency.

CAMERON DIAZ

Character contributes to beauty. It fortifies
a woman as her youth fades. A mode of
conduct, a standard of courage, discipline,
fortitude, and integrity can do a great deal
to make a woman beautiful.

AUTHOR UNKNOWN

inner beauty

> The most glorious sight that one ever sees beneath the stars
> is the sight of worthy Motherhood.
>
> GEORGE W. TRUETT

Iris

A beautiful purple *Iris* is a very regal looking flower and traditionally, it has been used to represent royalty. It illustrates for us the noble position of a Mother as the "queen" of her home...a role that requires her to use all of her inner resources to rule with wisdom and love. She is *honored* and respected by those she loves and serves.

honor

No person was ever honored for what he received. HONOR has been the reward for what he gave.
CALVIN COOLIDGE

$\mathcal{T}$he noblest calling in the world is that of Mother... She who rears successfully a family of healthy, beautiful sons and daughters whose immortal souls will be exerting an influence throughout the ages...deserves the highest *honor* that man can give.

David O. McKay

Being a Mother is so much more than giving birth. It takes all your time, energy, wit and strength, not to mention the wisdom and grace of God to see that a child succeeds.

Johnnie Walker

Dignity does not consist in possessing HONORS, but in deserving them.

ARISTOTLE

honor

A Mother is the one who is still there
when everyone else has deserted you.

AUTHOR UNKNOWN

Sweet Pea

Sweet Peas have little curling tendrils that love to hug things and never let go, reminding us that a Mother's love is very nurturing with lots of hugs and tender loving care... and it never lets go... A Mother's love is forever.

However time or circumstance may come between a Mother and her child, their lives are interwoven forever.

PAM BROWN

forever

A Mother knits the family together with the threads of honor and respect, weaves their lives together with nurture and care, and holds them all tightly with bonds of love and prayer.

AUTHOR UNKNOWN

A Mother holds her children's hands for a while, but their hearts forever.

AUTHOR UNKNOWN

Sometimes I wonder... What kind of example am I leaving my children? What will they write on my tombstone or say about me after I'm gone?... Hopefully my epitaph will read something like this: "She hated folding laundry but liked to fold us in her arms."

Dena Dyer

In the depth of winter I finally learned
that within me there lay an invincible summer.

ALBERT CAMUS

Daffodil

The *Daffodil* is one of the first bulbs to burst through the cold winter ground, sometimes through the snow itself … and like a beautiful little trumpet, it heralds the coming of spring. It represents fresh hope and is a picture of the Mother who is able to live confidently through the bleak and difficult winter seasons of her life, because she maintains an attitude of optimism and faith.

Hope is a state of mind, not of the world. Hope, in this deep and powerful sense, is not the same as joy that things are going well, or willingness to invest in enterprises that are obviously heading for success, but rather an ability to work for something because it is good.

VACLAV HAVEL

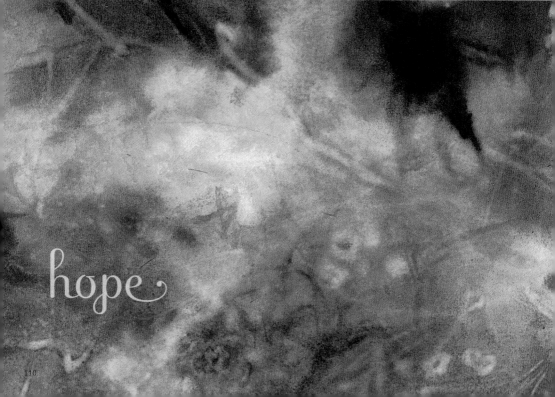

HOPE, like the gleaming taper's light,
adorns and cheers our way; And still,
as darker grows the night,
emits a brighter ray.

OLIVER GOLDSMITH

hope

$\mathcal{L}$ive for today but hold your hands open to tomorrow. Anticipate the future and its changes with joy. There is a seed of God's love in every event, every circumstance, every unpleasant situation in which you may find yourself.

Barbara Johnson

Love recognizes no barriers. It jumps hurdles, leaps fences, penetrates walls to arrive at its destination full of *hope*.

MAYA ANGELOU

I believe that there is no greater good in all the world than Motherhood.
The INFLUENCE of a Mother in the lives of her children is beyond calculation.

JAMES E. FAUST

Cornflower

The *Cornflower* is a very small flower, but God gave
it a special brilliant blue color. This little flower reminds us that every Mother, no matter how small
and insignificant she may feel, can have a tremendous *influence* in the lives of her children and
make a difference in their world.

Motherhood is the greatest potential **influence** *in human society.
Her caress first awakens in the child a sense of security; her kiss the
first realization of affection; her sympathy and tenderness, the first
assurance that there is love in the world. Thus in infancy and
childhood she implants ever-directing and restraining
influences that remain through life.*

DAVID O. MCKAY

influence

To be a Mother is a woman's greatest vocation in life.
She is a partner with God. No being has a position of such
power and influence. She holds in her hands the destiny
of nations, for to her comes the responsibility and
opportunity of molding the nation's citizens.

SPENCER W. KIMBALL

Mothers have as powerful an INFLUENCE
over the welfare of future generations as
all other earthly causes combined.

SIR JOHN S. C. ABBOTT

A hundred years from now it will not matter
what my bank account was, the sort of house I
lived in, or the kind of car I drove, but the world
may be different because I was important in the
life of a child.

Forest E. Witcraft

Gerbera Daisy

A Mother's love lays a foundation for success.
A Mother's encouragement builds the CONFIDENCE to succeed.

AUTHOR UNKNOWN

A single stem *Gerbera Daisy* is strong enough to stand alone and looks beautiful all by itself in a vase. It represents the Mother who gives her children the strength and confidence they need to walk alone and stand tall in the world ... to follow their dreams ... and to become the best version of themselves.

The doctors told me that I would never walk, but my Mother told me I would, so I believed my Mother.

WILMA RUDOLPH *(Olympic runner)*

$\mathcal{I}$f you would have your son to walk
honorably through the world, you must not
attempt to clear the stones from his path, but teach him
to walk firmly over them ... not insist upon leading him
by the hand, but let him learn to go alone.

ANNE BRONTE

❧

My Mother said to me,
"If you become a soldier, you'll be a general;
if you become a monk, you'll end up as the pope."
Instead, I was a painter and became Picasso.

PABLO PICASSO

My Mother gave me the courage to pursue my dreams,

making me believe in myself and that I could achieve

anything I put my mind to, as long as I worked hard enough

SARAH FRASE

confidence

A Mother is a treasure, more precious than Gold. . .
for love shared is PRICELESS and never grows old.

AUTHOR UNKNOWN

Chrysanthemum

The name *Chrysanthemum* comes from two Greek words... *chrysos* (gold) and *anthos* (flower)—"*gold flower*"—reminding us of the purity and strength of a Mother's love. It is like fine gold... extraordinary in beauty... *priceless* and able to stand the test of time.

A Mother is not to be compared to any other person – she is incomparable.

AFRICAN PROVERB

Nurturing care...

discipline & laughter...

the encouragement of dreams...

these are the *priceless* gifts

of a Mother's love.

AUTHOR UNKNOWN

The little things that make life sweet
are worth their weight in gold;
They can't be bought at any price
and neither are they sold.

ESTELLE WAITE HOOVER

$\mathcal{M}$otherhood is priced of God,

at a price no man may dare to lessen

or misunderstand.

Helen Hunt Jackson

priceless

> The Mother is and must be, whether she knows it or not,
> the greatest, strongest, and most lasting
> teacher her children have.
>
> HANNAH WHITALL SMITH

Aster

The *Aster* is sometimes called "star flower" because the name comes from the Greek word for *star*. This flower reminds us that a Mother is a bright star in her children's lives that guides them through their journey of life. As their primary teacher from birth, she bears the responsibility for giving them the tools they need to be successful, caring adults.

The Mother's heart is the child's schoolroom.

HENRY WARD BEECHER

What we teach our children today will be the values that sustain them in their future.

CYNDI BIXLER

Give your children enough guidance
to lead them in the right direction.
Give yourself enough restraint to let
them become their own people.

AUTHOR UNKNOWN

To bring up a child in the way he should go…
travel that way yourself.

JOSH BILLINGS

If your children enter adulthood

with a clear concept of who God is

and what He wants them to do,

you will have achieved the

greatest accomplishments in life.

DR. JAMES DOBSON

Easter Lily

The *Easter Lily* symbolizes a *fresh start* ... a new beginning ... as the dead bulbs planted in the winter become beautiful flowers in the springtime. It represents the Mother who believes in the best for each of her children and is always willing to give them another chance to start over. She has unlimited patience and perseverance ... always hoping, always believing ... that each child has the potential to succeed and will accomplish his or her dreams.

Don't drag yesterday's problems into this brand new day. Give yourself, and those around you, a break ... start fresh.

LUCY MACDONALD

My Mother never gave up on me. I messed up in school so much they were sending me home, but my Mother sent me right back.

DENZEL WASHINGTON

Isn't it nice to think that tomorrow is a new day with no mistakes in it yet?

L.M. MONTGOMERY *(Anne of Green Gables)*

I have always been delighted at the prospect of a new day, a *fresh try*, one more start, with perhaps a bit of magic waiting somewhere behind the morning!

JOSEPH PRIESTLEY

fresh start

With the new day comes new strength and new thoughts.

ELEANOR ROOSEVELT

My Mom is a never-ending song in my heart of comfort, happiness, and being.
I may sometimes forget the words but I always remember the tune.

GRAYCIE HARMON

Carnation

The name *Carnation* is one of the most common and least expensive of the cut flowers, and yet its fragrance is one of the sweetest and lasts even after the flower has died. It represents for us the tremendous significance of a woman's life as a Mother. She makes a difference in her world by touching the lives of those she loves with a beautiful fragrance that will continue on after she is gone.

*All that is purest and best in man is but
the echo of a Mother's benediction.*

FREDERICK W. MORTON

*It is only in after life that men gaze
backward and behold how a Mother's
hand and heart of LOVE molded their
young lives and shaped their destiny.*

E.W. CASWELL

significance

$\mathcal{Y}$ou will find as you look back upon your life that the moments when you have really lived, are the moments when you have done things in a spirit of love.

Henry Drummond

You don't get to choose how you're going to die…
You can only choose how you're going to live.

JOAN BAEZ

The best use of life is LOVE.
The best expression of love is TIME.
The best time to love is NOW.

RICK WARREN

Heart of a Mother

A *Mother* is born in that very moment
a child becomes her own.
And her *heart* begins to overflow
with a love she has never known.

Her focus changes instantly
as her *heart* beats for another.
It will never be the same again.
It's the powerful heart of a mother!

It's a *heart* of incredible courage
with strength and endurance too.
She fiercely protects and defends her young
in ways only love can do.

She sacrifices "self" to give
her children what they need,
developing their character
to make sure that they succeed.

Just like a lovely gardener
she plants her seeds of *love.*
Her *heart* gives lots of sunshine
like blessings from above.

She provides a firm foundation ...
a peaceful, loving home
So her children's roots run deep and strong
no matter where they roam.

With a *heart* that nurtures them along
to grow in the right direction
She allows them freedom to blossom and thrive
under her wise protection.

They're prepared to face the storms of life,
as they learn to stand alone.
She gives them a sense of value and strength
with a confidence of their own.

There's a special beauty in a *Mother's love*
She's a picture of wisdom and grace
We honor her with gratitude ...

No one can take her place!

PAULA J. FOX

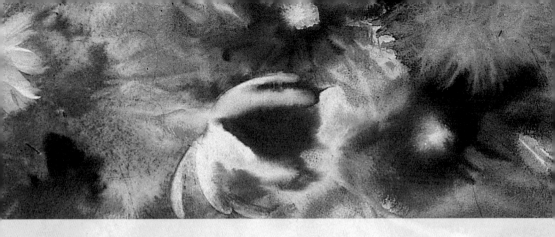

$\mathcal{M}$others are the first book read,
and the last put aside in every child's library.

C. LENOX REDMOND

About the Author

Paula J. Fox describes herself as a lifetime student whose passion is to continue learning and applying godly wisdom in her life so that she can share it with others. Her desire is to inspire and motivate others to live a life of purpose and significance. She is a teacher at heart with a degree in special education and 35 years of experience teaching and leading all ages from preschool through adult.

She and her husband, Larry, have three grown children and she is now able to devote more of her time to writing. Besides being a teacher and leader in her own church, she is the founder and leader of L'dor *(Ladies' day of renewal)*, a home-based Bible study for women. This ministry, which began over 25 years ago, meets weekly in homes where they worship together through songs and scriptures, sharing and studying God's Word together. Paula loves researching and writing her own lessons for L'dor as well as writing poetry and prose. She also enjoys speaking to women's groups and retreats.

Paula J. Fox is the author of several Simple Truths books including:

Heart of a Teacher,
Mothers Are Heaven's Scent,
The Second Mile.
and *Heart of a Caregiver.*

You may contact Paula J. Fox at:
paulajfox@live.com

simple truths®
Motivational & Inspirational Gifts

If you have enjoyed this book we invite you to check out our entire collection of gift books, with free inspirational movies, at **www.simpletruths.com.**

You'll discover it's a great way to inspire *friends* and *family*, or to *thank* your best customers and employees.